The Heart of Route 66

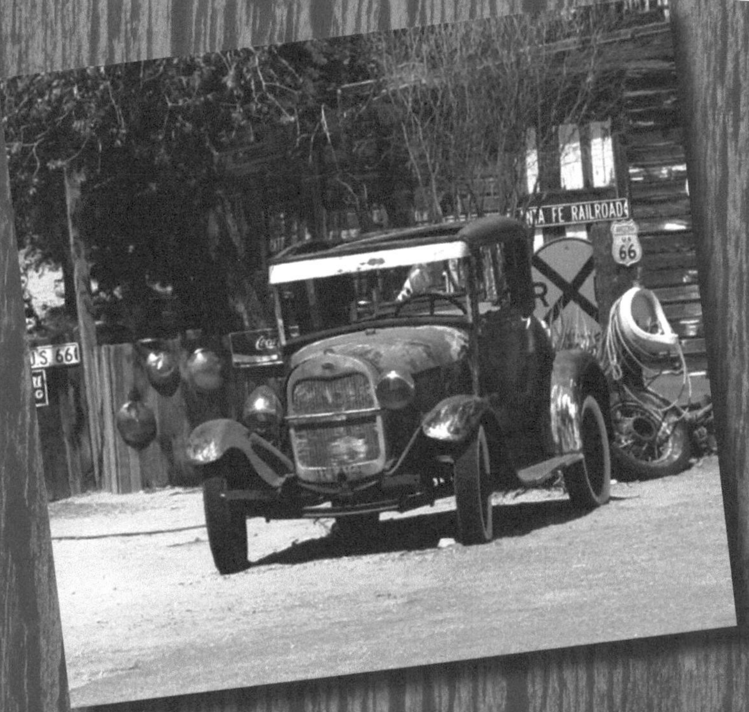

Photographed by

Herb Schroeder

AuthorHouse™
1663 Liberty Drive, Suite 200
Bloomington, IN 47403
www.authorhouse.com
Phone: 1-800-839-8640

authorHOUSE

Printed in the United States of America
Bloomington, Indiana

This book is printed on acid-free paper.

First published by AuthorHouse 4/16/2008

ISBN: 978-1-4343-8136-1 (sc)

Library of Congress Control Number: 2008903642

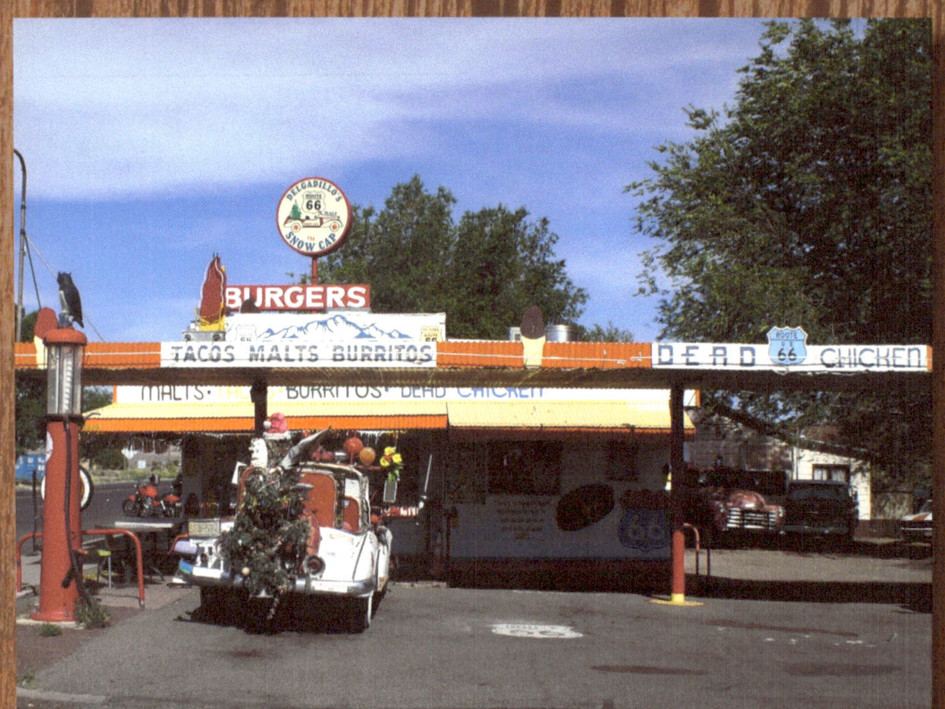

The Snow Cap started by Juan Delgadillo in Seligman, Arizona.

Juan and his brother Angel were founding members of the Route 66 Association.

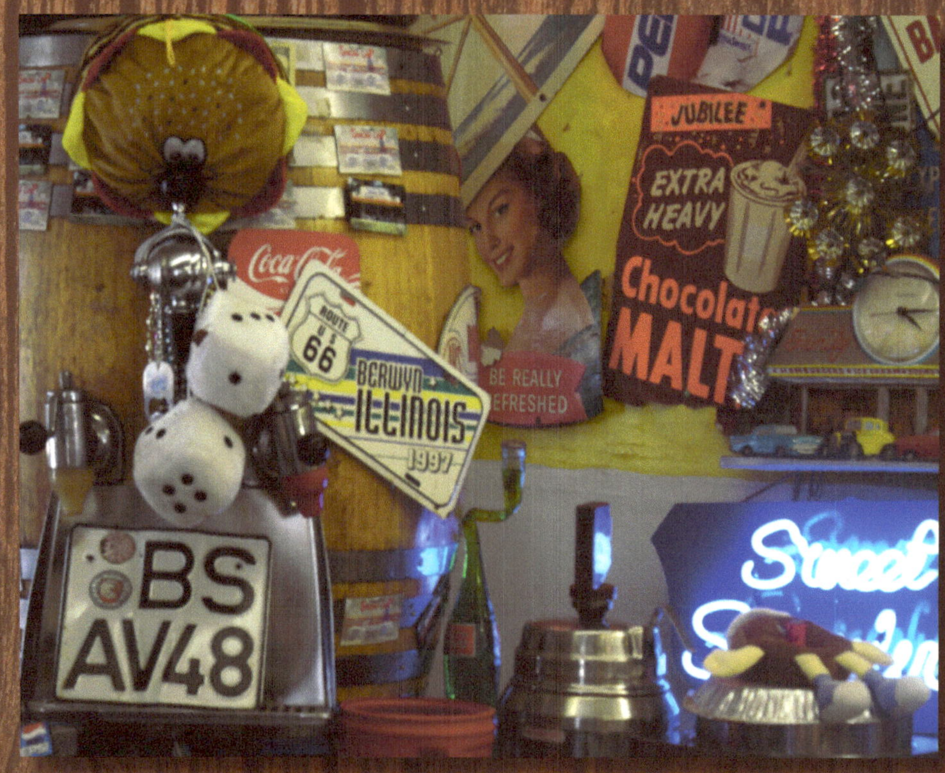

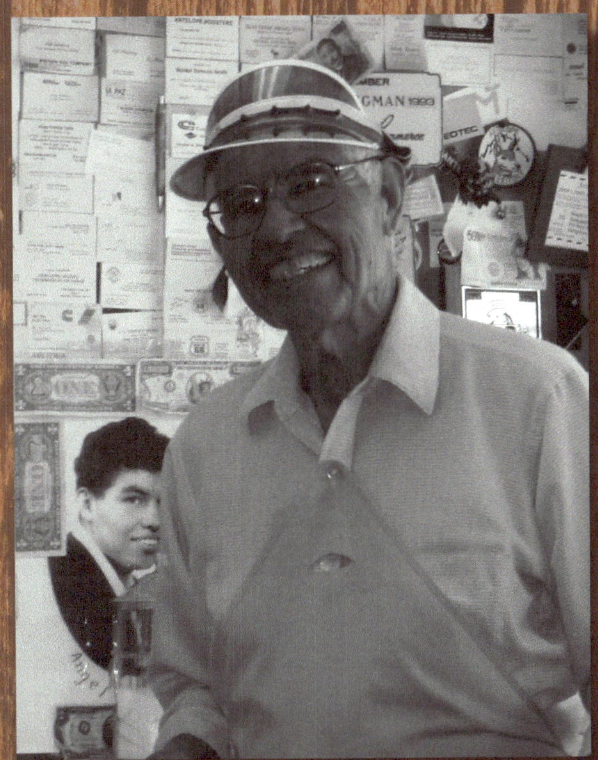

Mr. Angel Delgadillo.

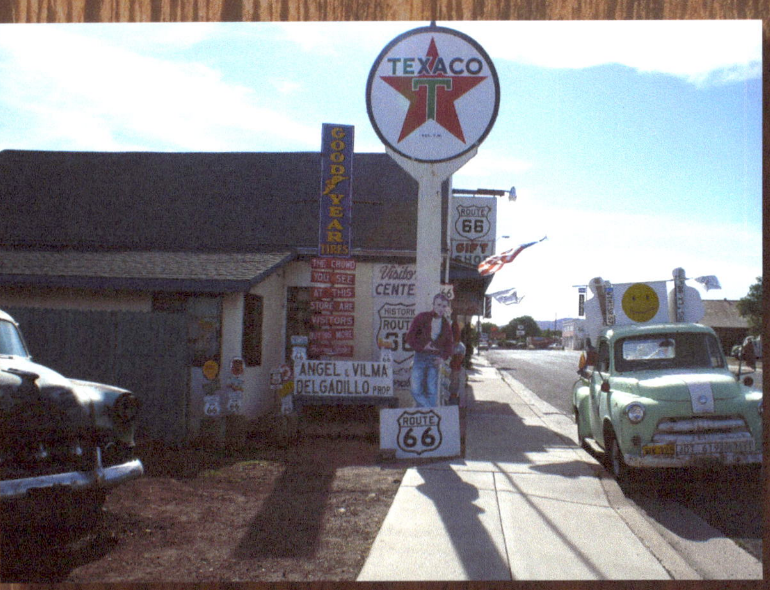

Angel's BarberShop/Souvenirs in Seligman, Arizona.

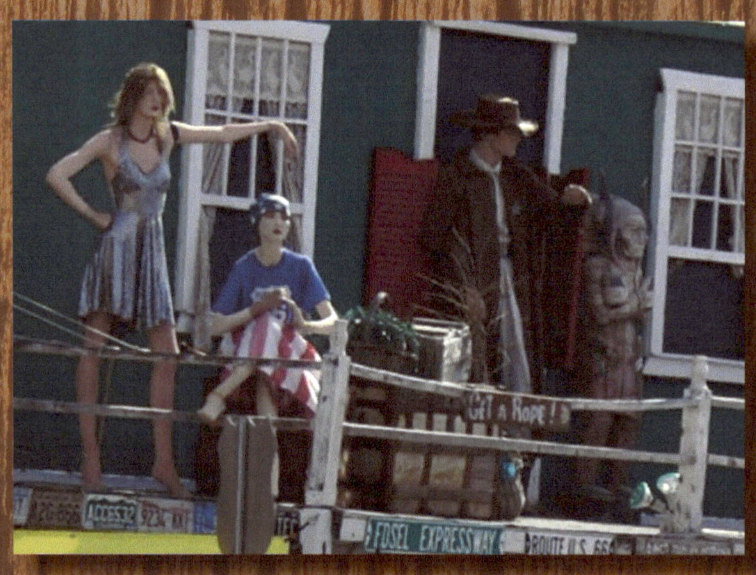

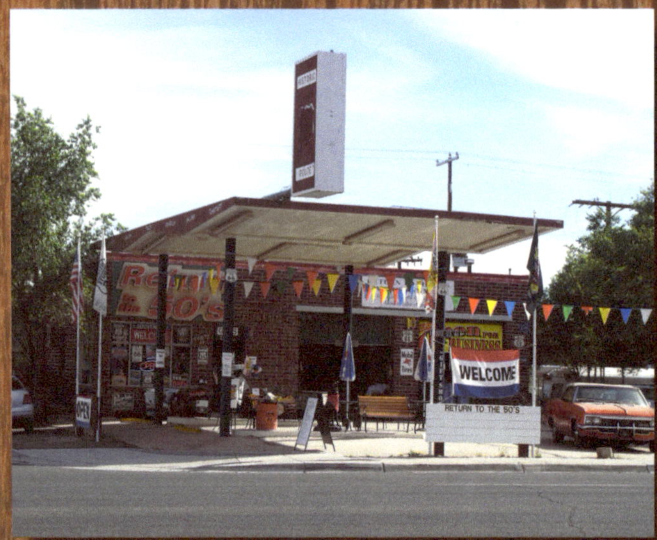

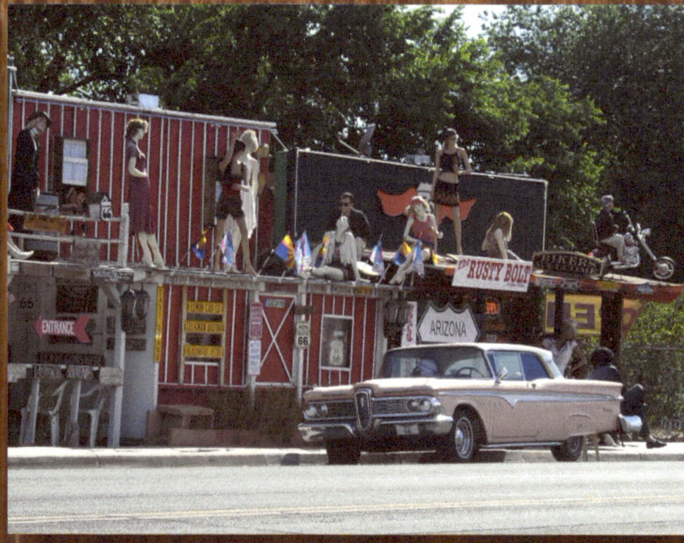

Some of the attractions in Seligman, Arizona.

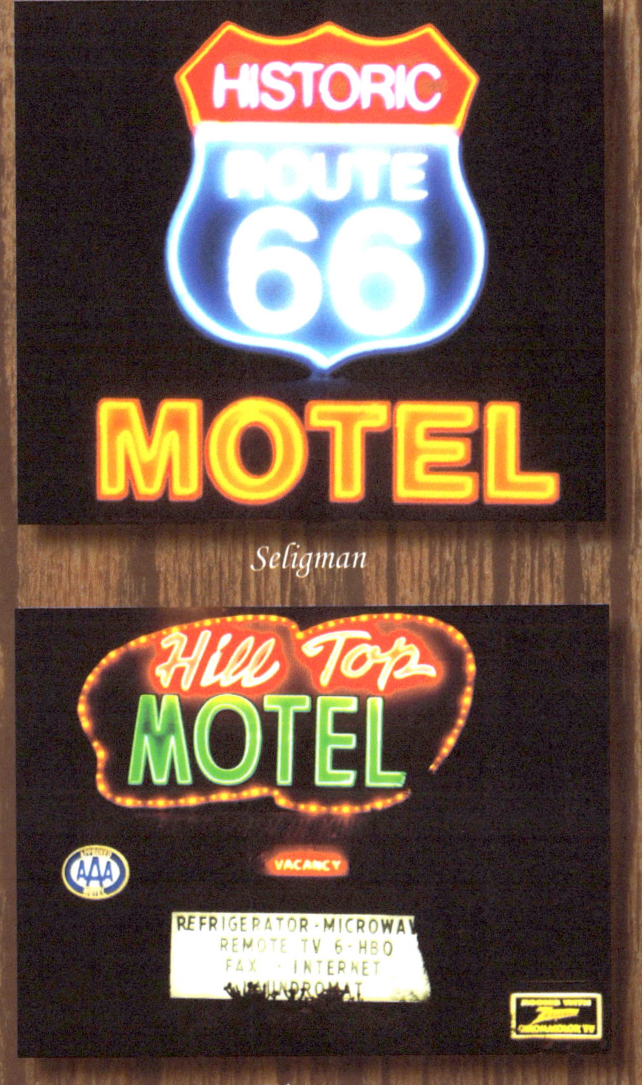

Seligman

Kingman

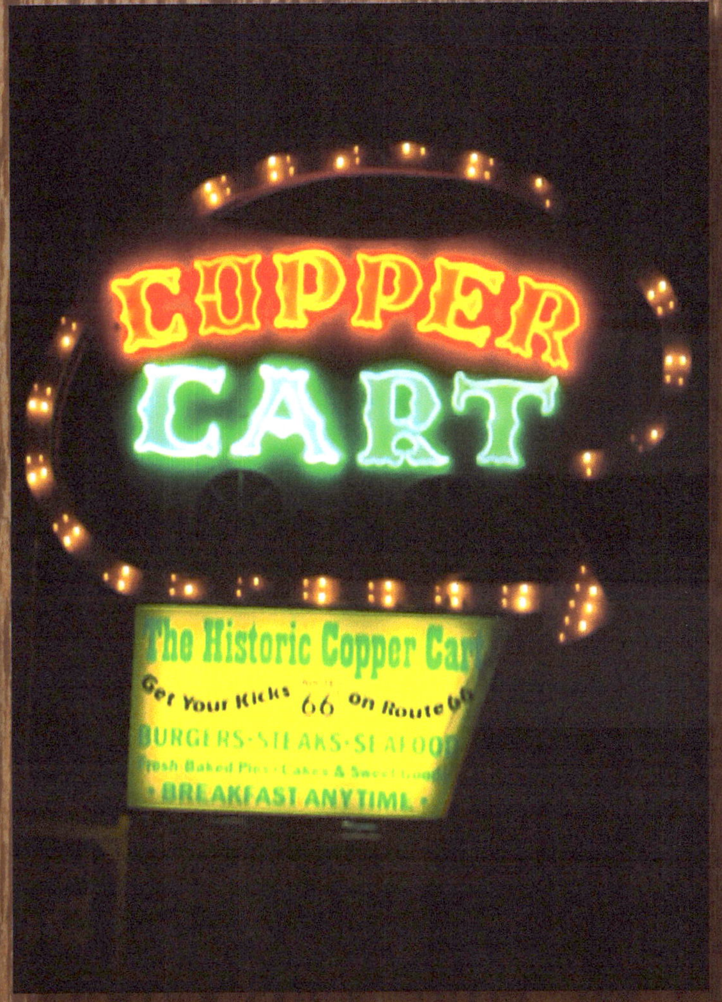

Seligman

There are some great neon signs that have survived along this stretch of road.

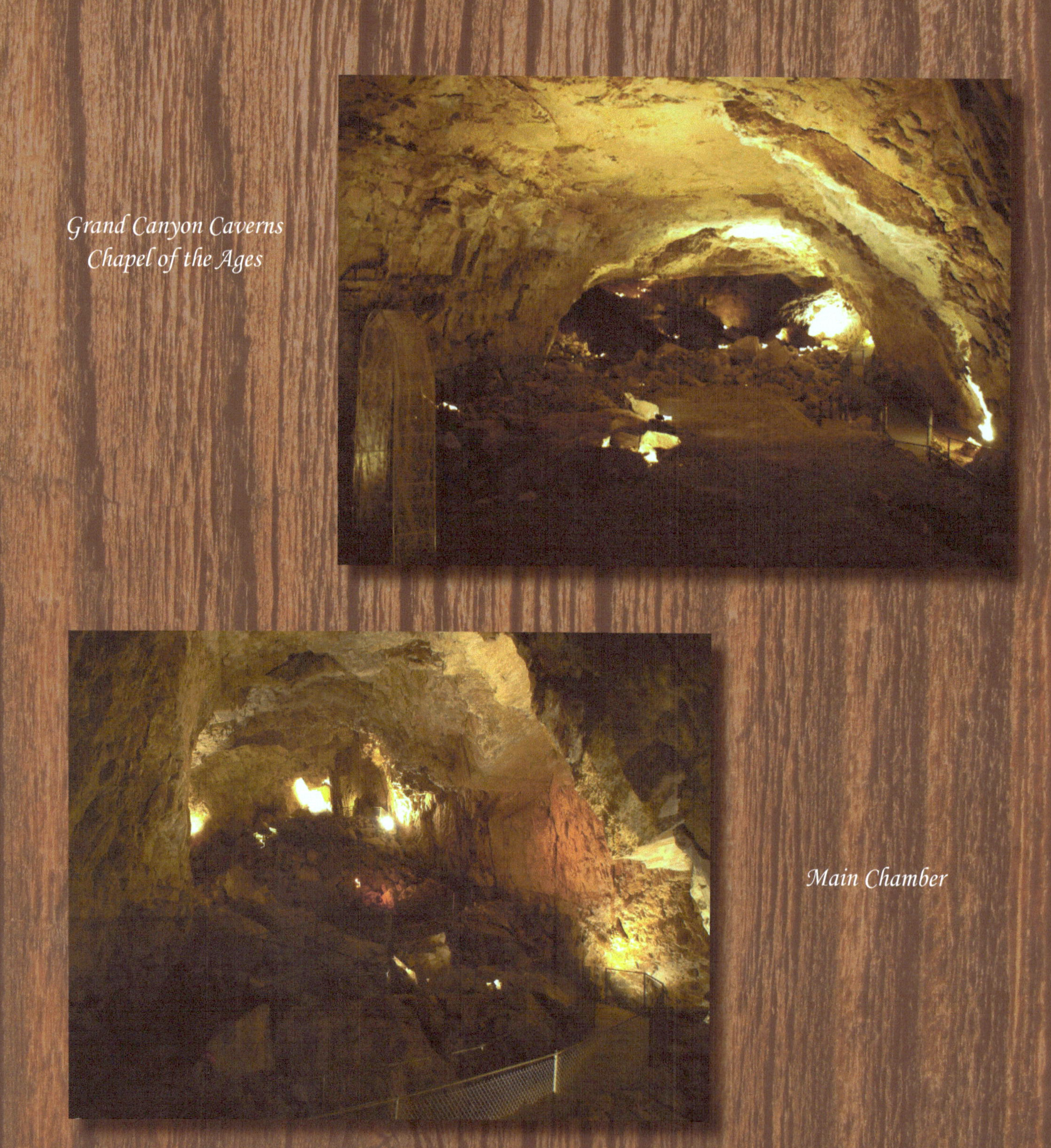

Grand Canyon Caverns
Chapel of the Ages

Main Chamber

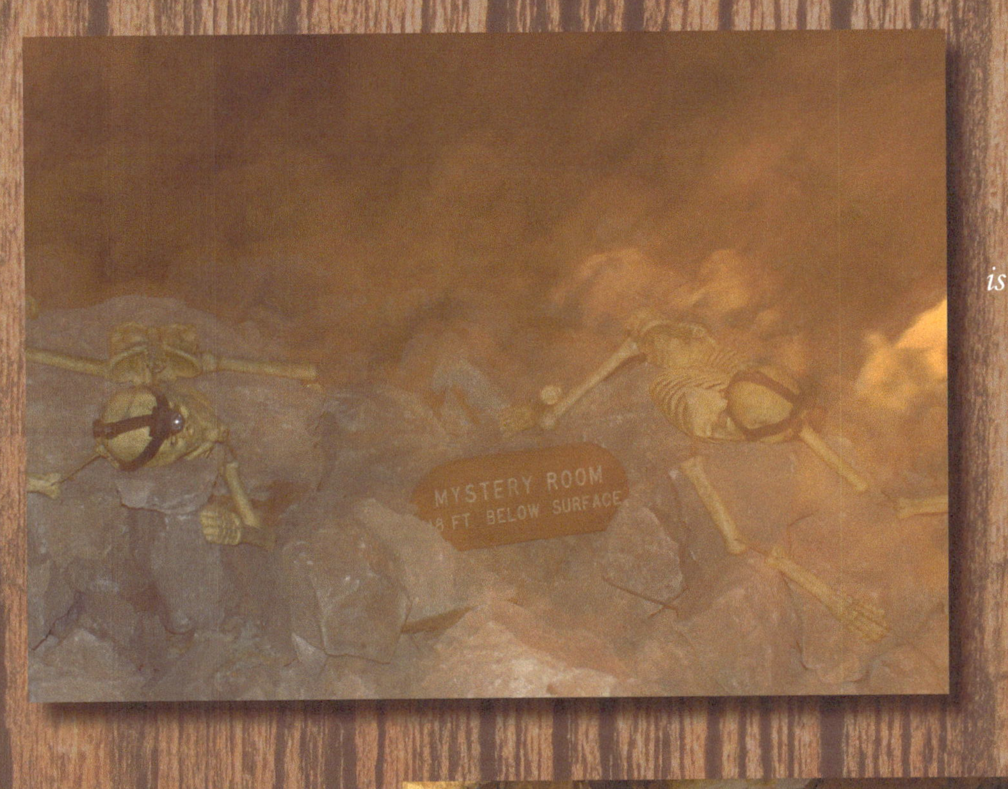

Just outside the
Mystery Room
is an interesting display

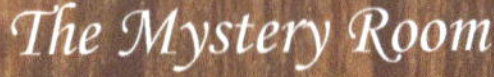

The Mystery Room

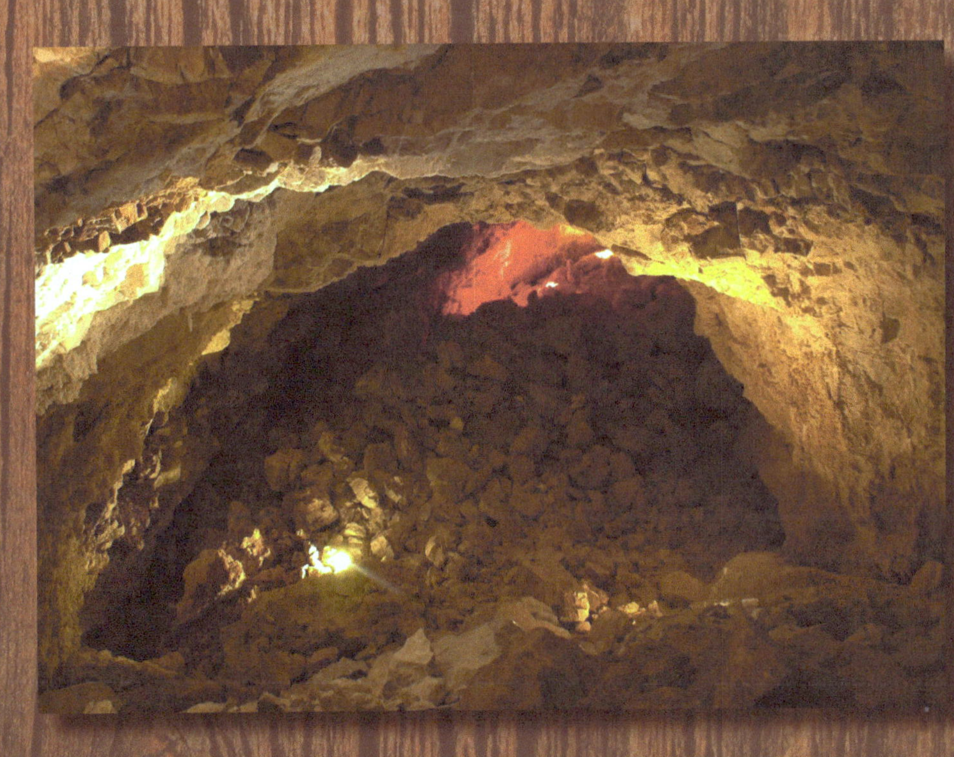

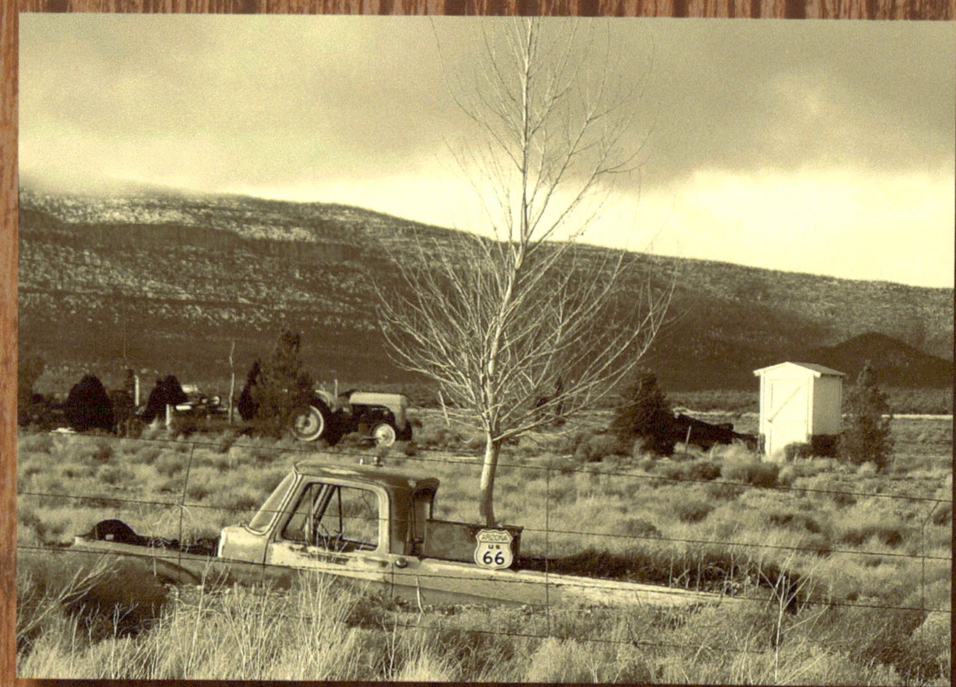

Truxton, Arizona.
There is a tree growing
in the Barrel.

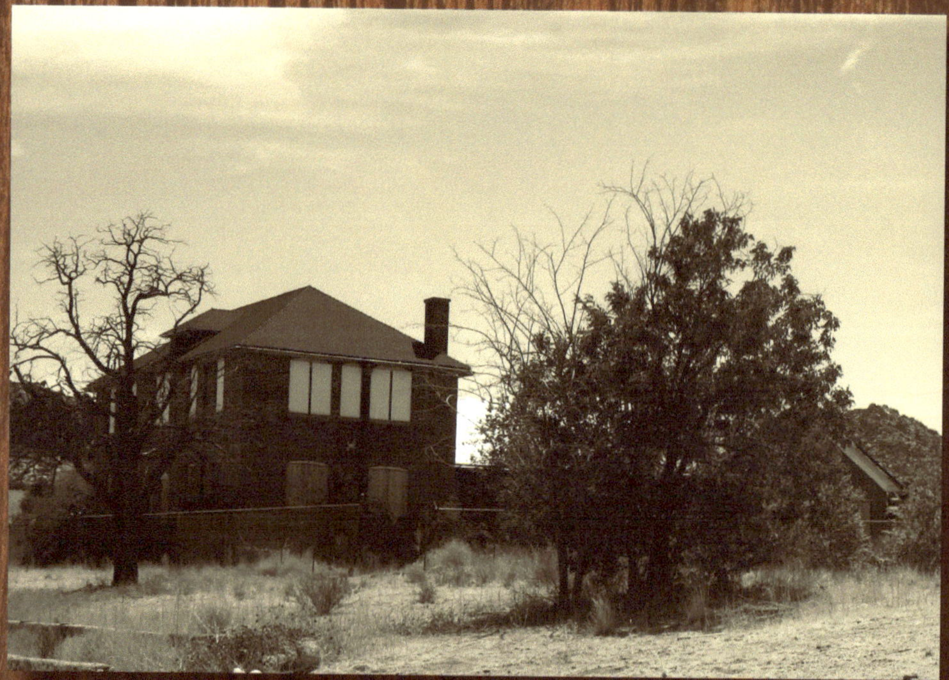

Old school house in
Valentine, Arizona.

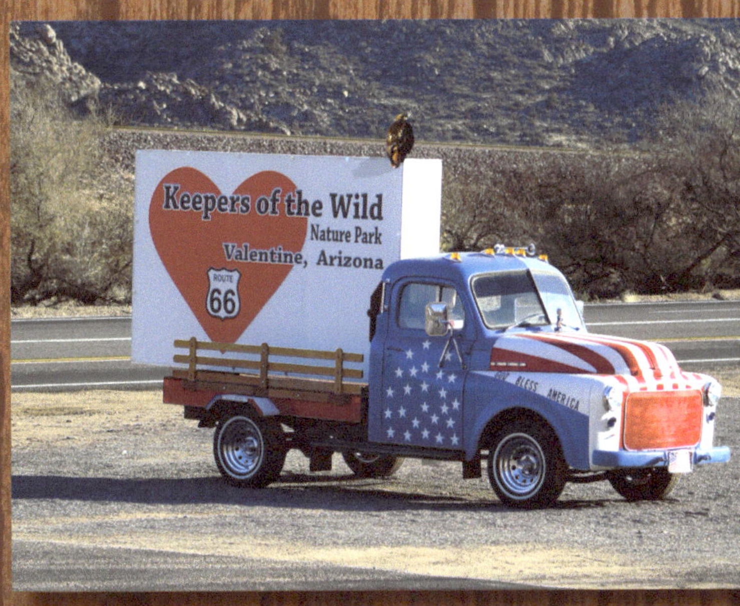

Lots of great animals to see.

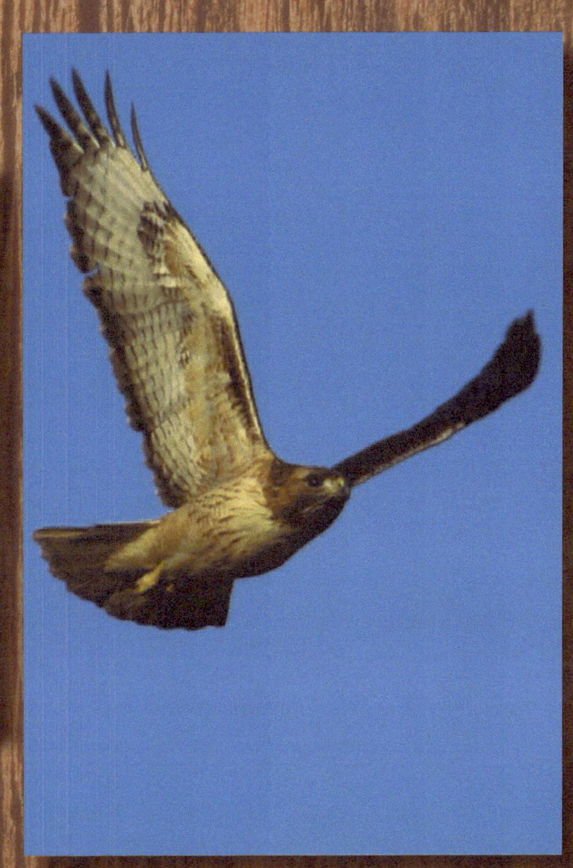

Red Tail Hawks are sometimes seen along the road.

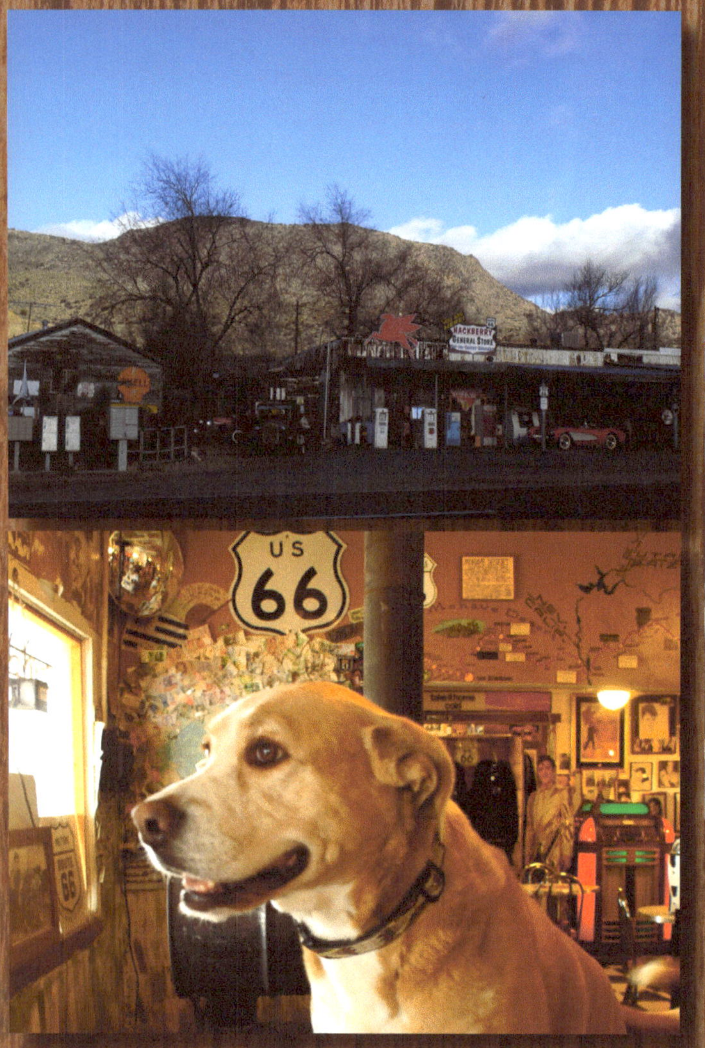

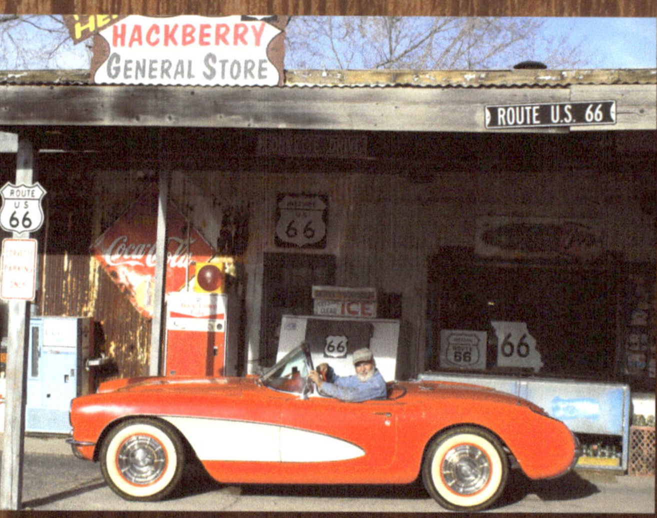

Mr. John Pritchard, owner of the Hackberry General Store and his dog Mr. Max, to the left

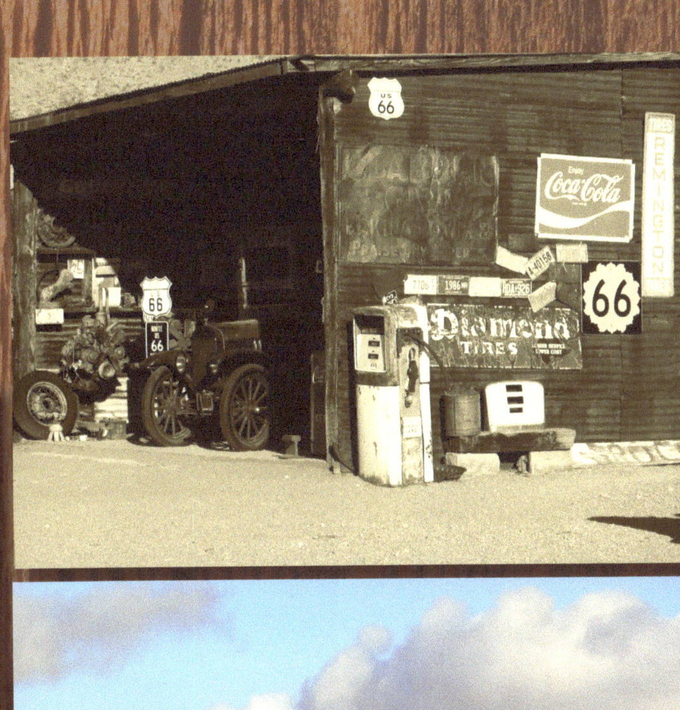

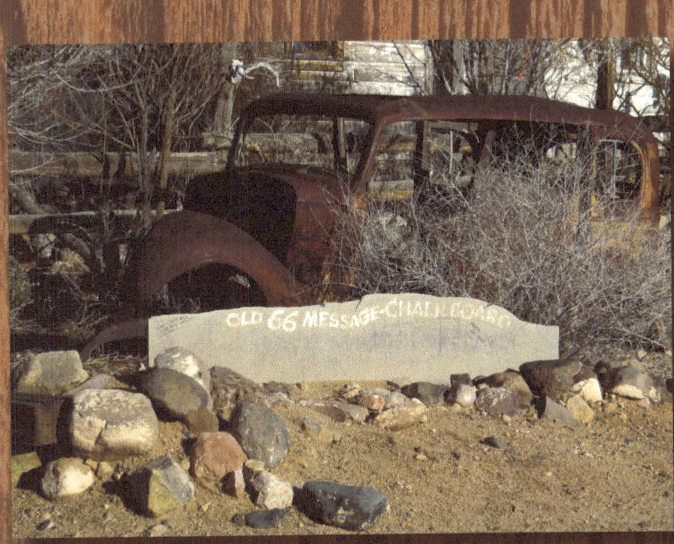

Lots of history to see, from the Heart of Route 66, at the Hackberry General Store.

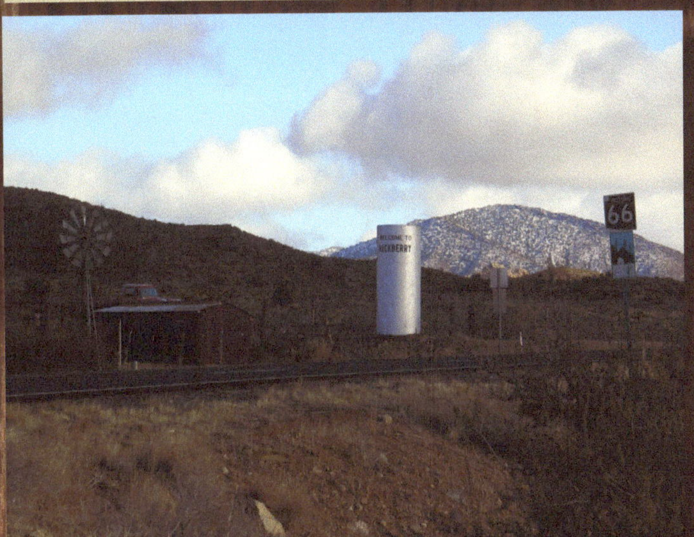

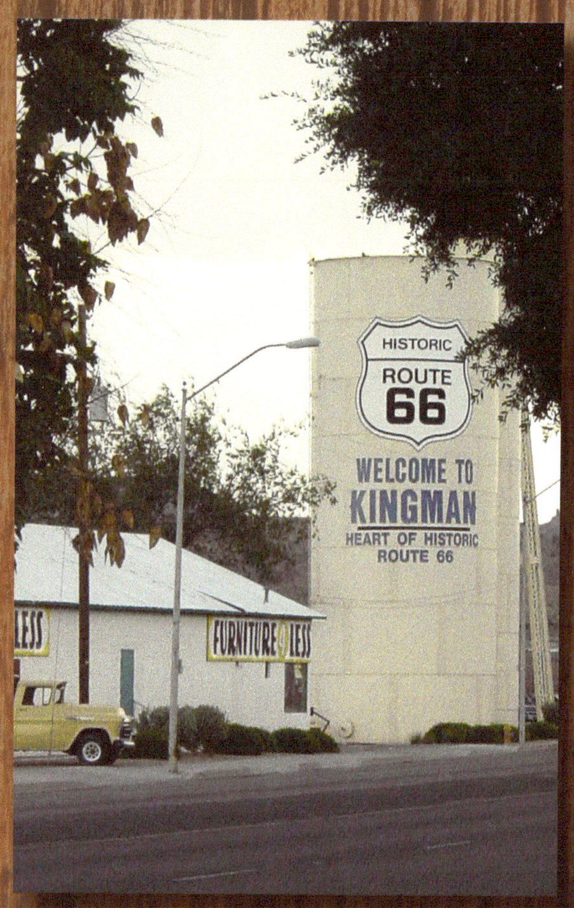

Downtown Kingman, Arizona.

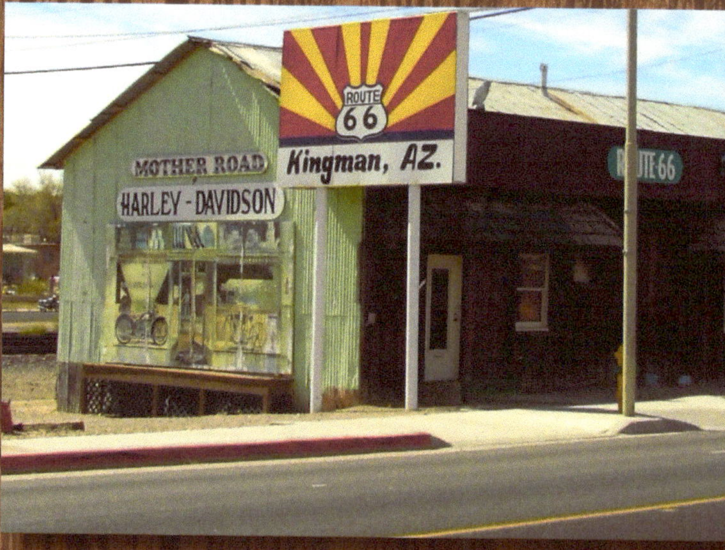

Kingman is proud of its Route 66 heritage.

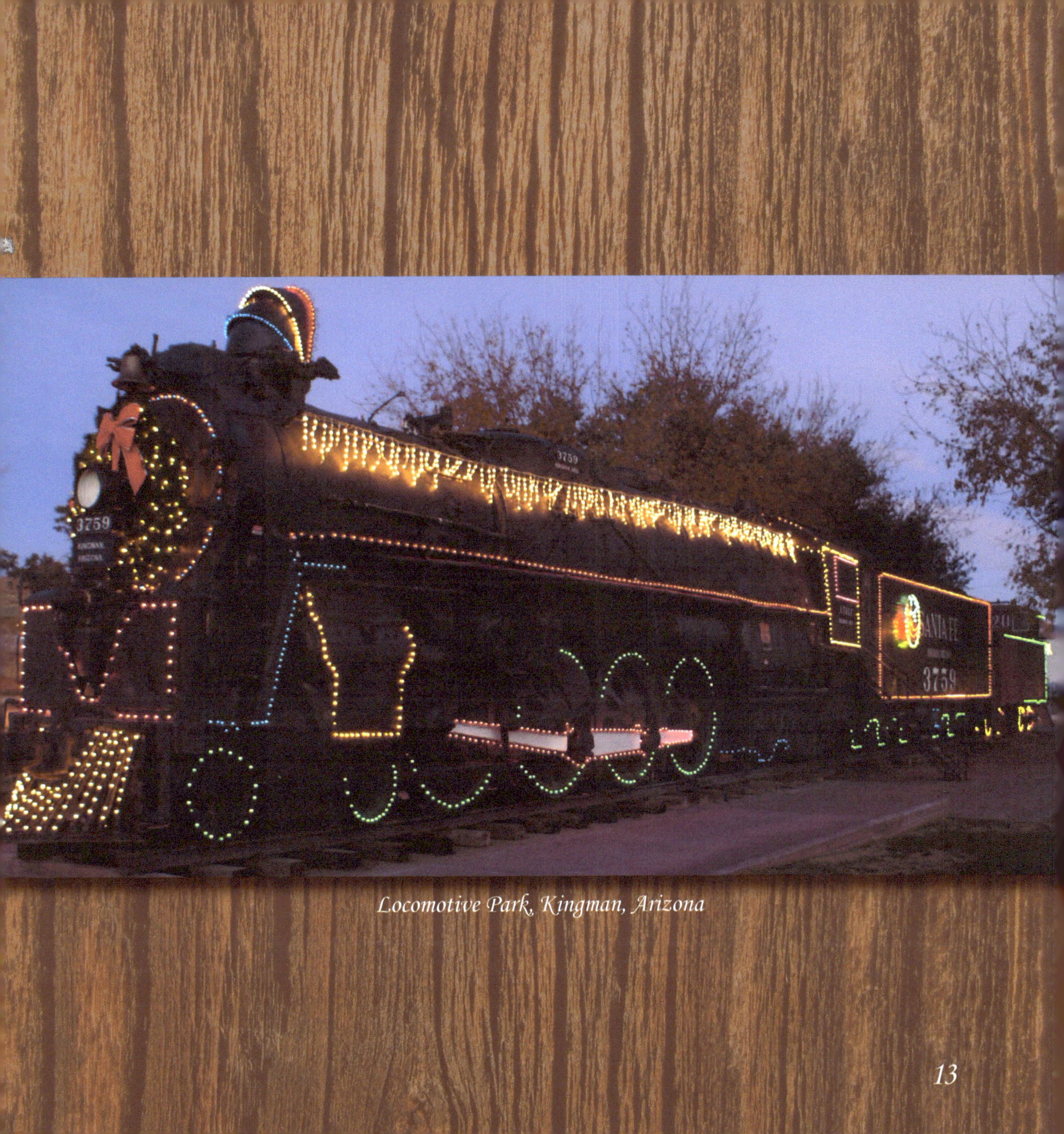

Locomotive Park, Kingman, Arizona

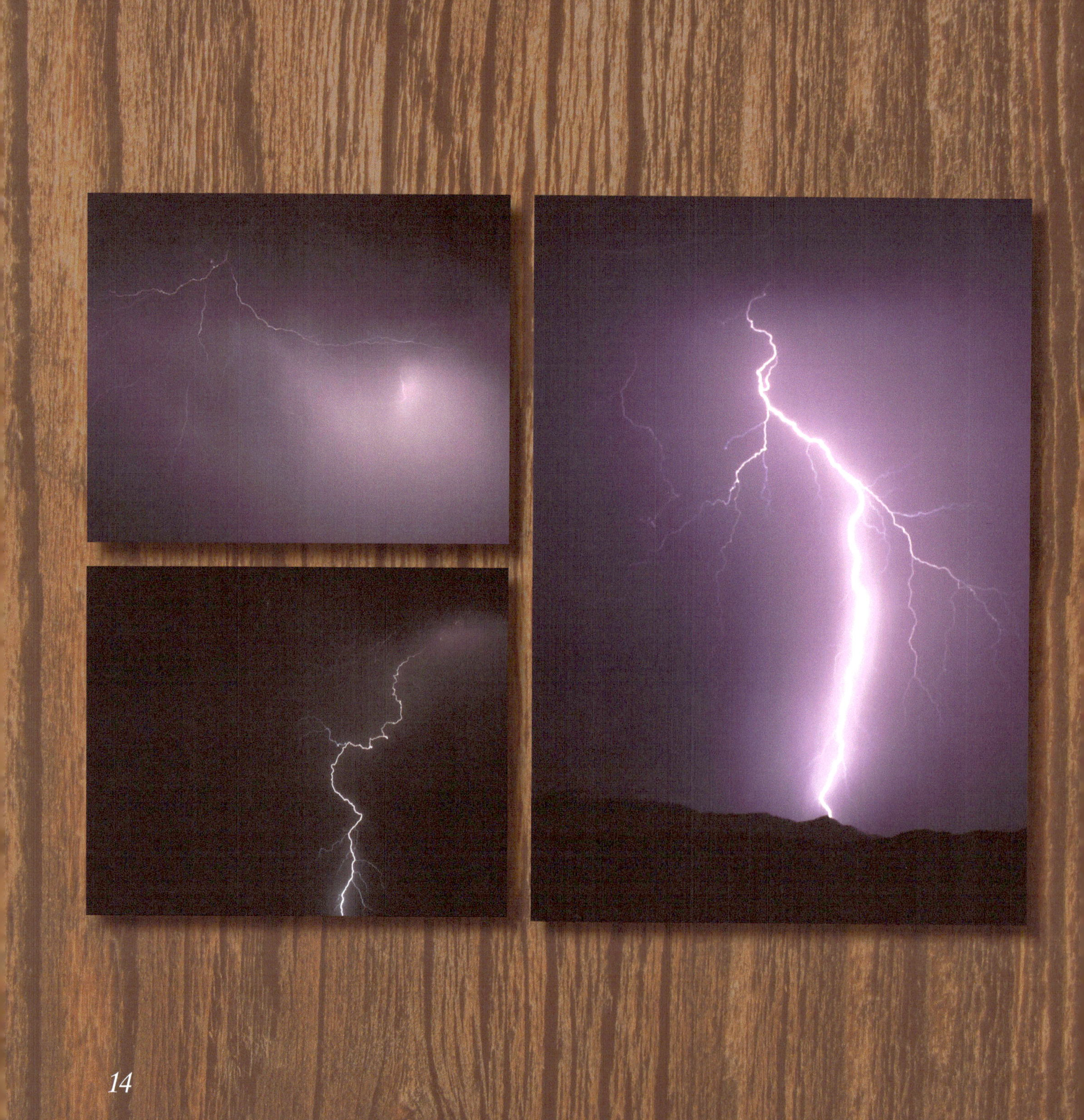

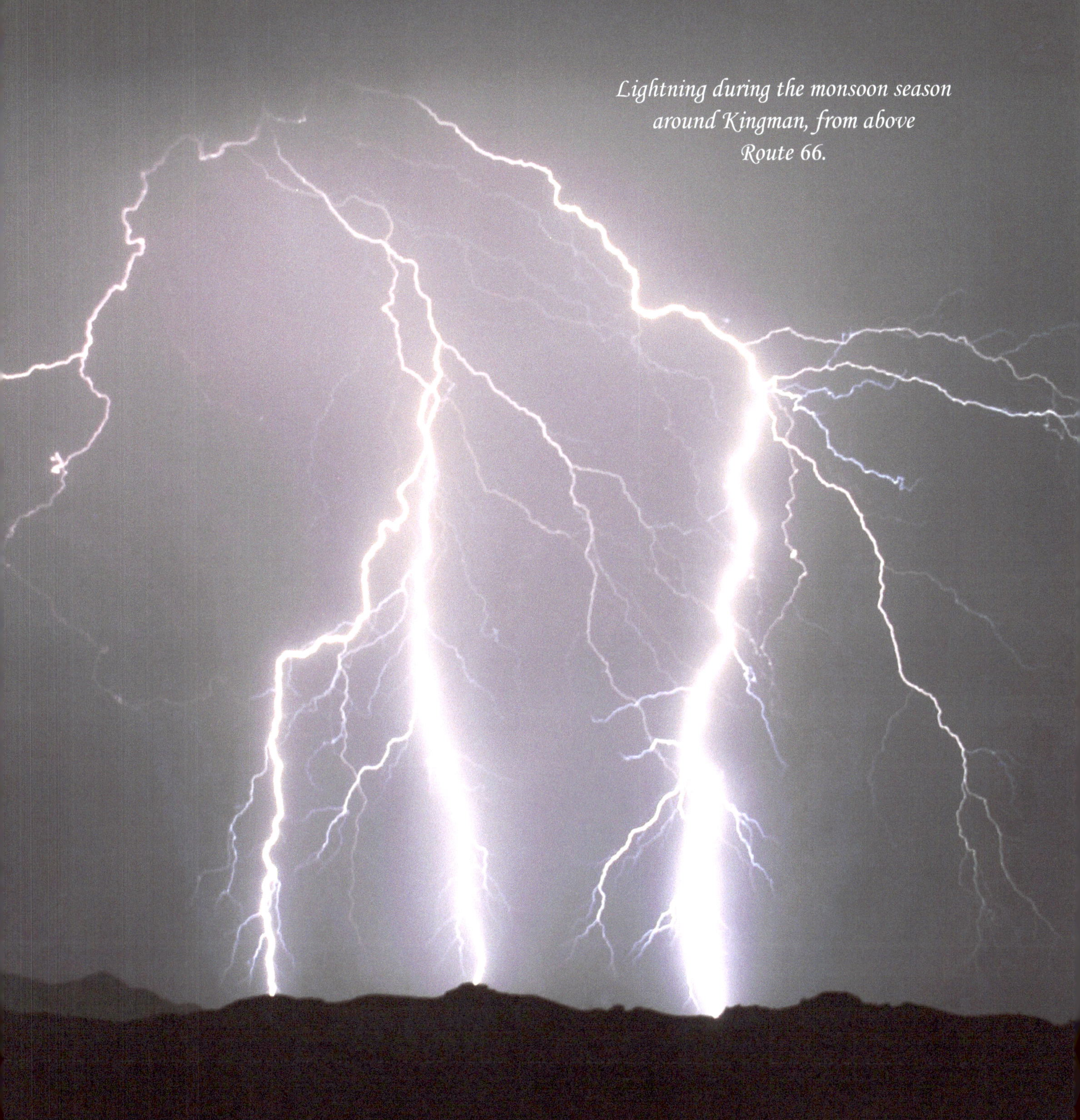

Lightning during the monsoon season around Kingman, from above Route 66.

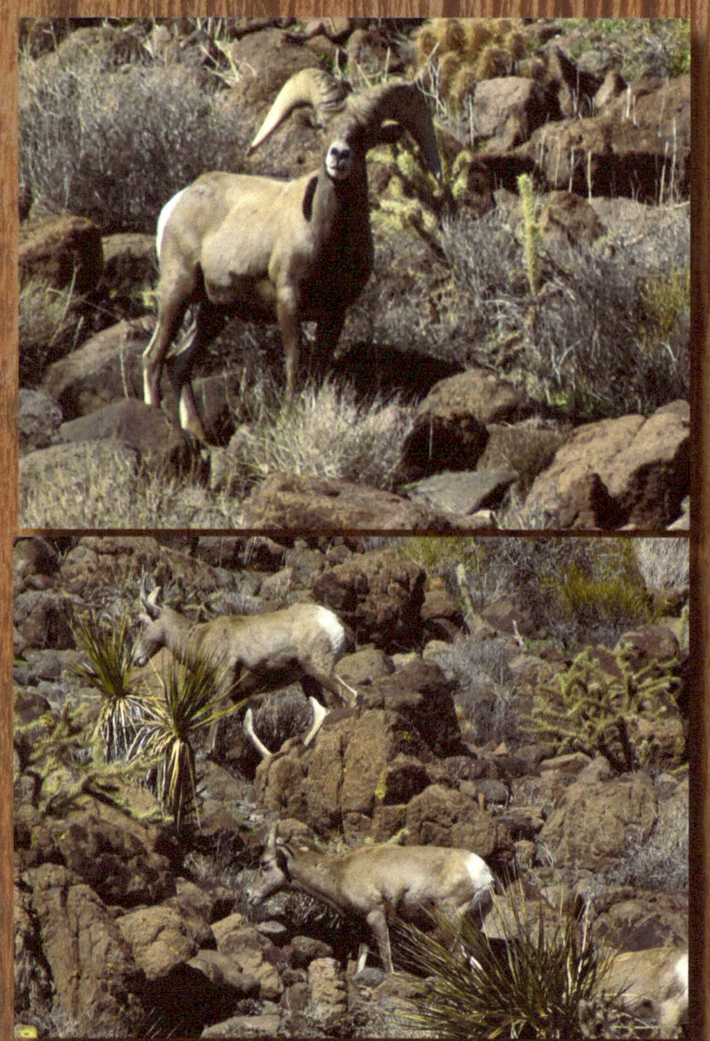

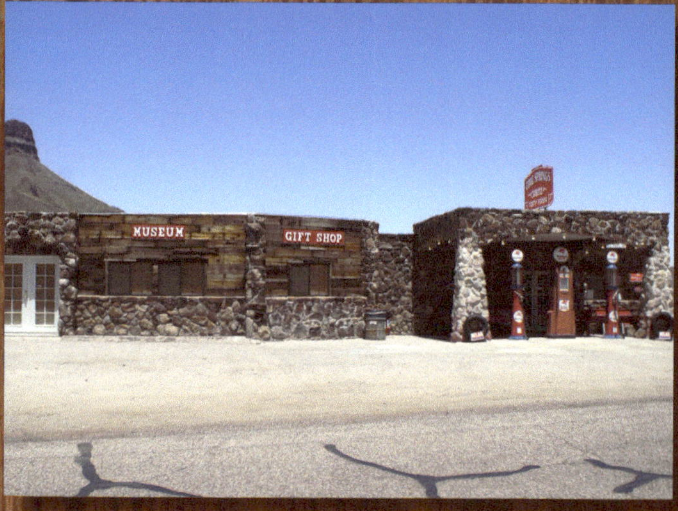

Cool Springs has been revitalized.
Left: Desert Big Horn Sheep grazing

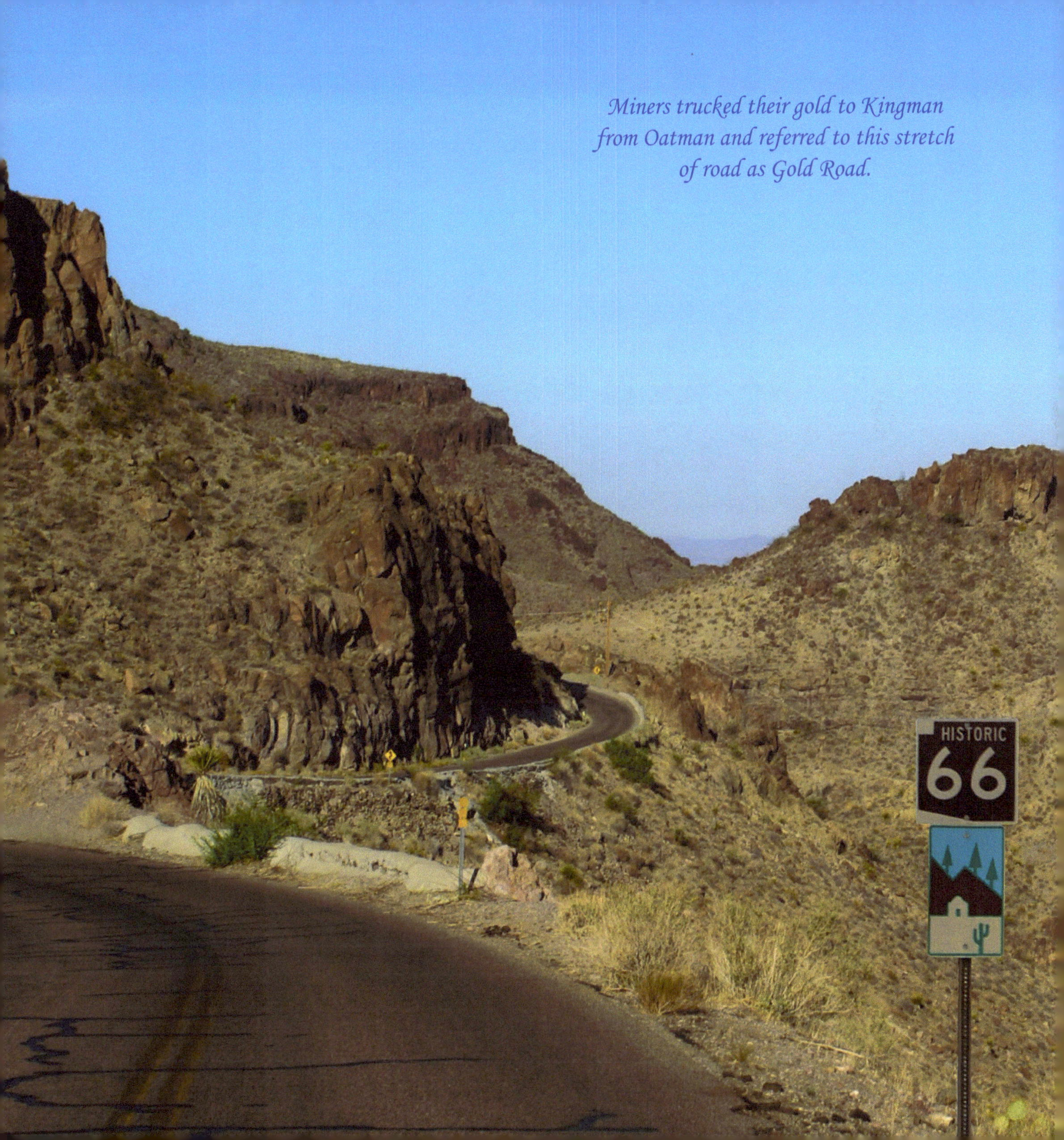

Miners trucked their gold to Kingman from Oatman and referred to this stretch of road as Gold Road.

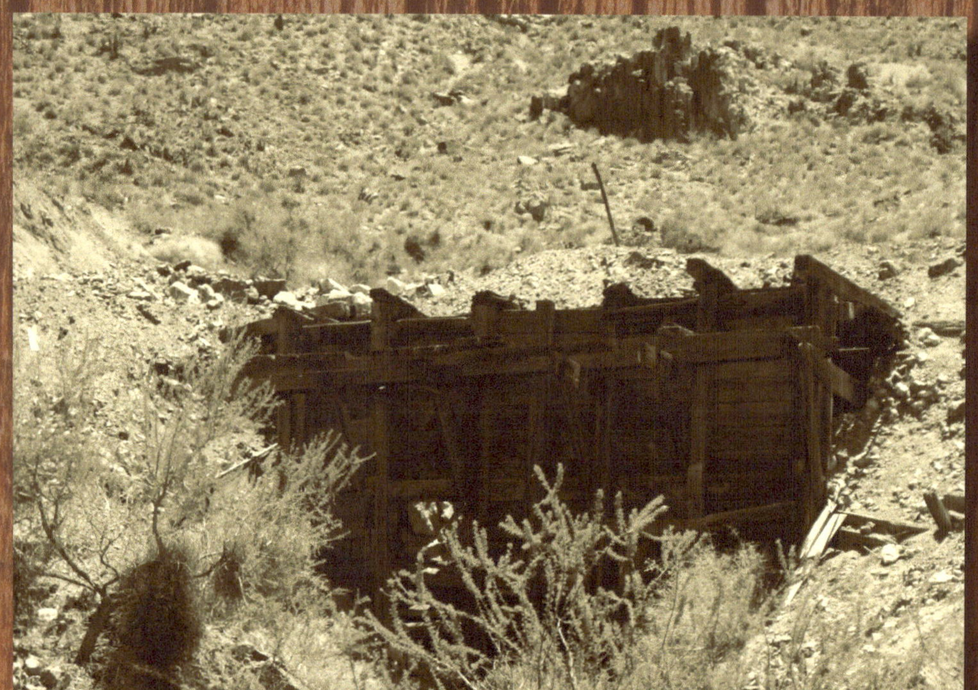

Mines and ruins along the Gold Road stretch of Route 66.

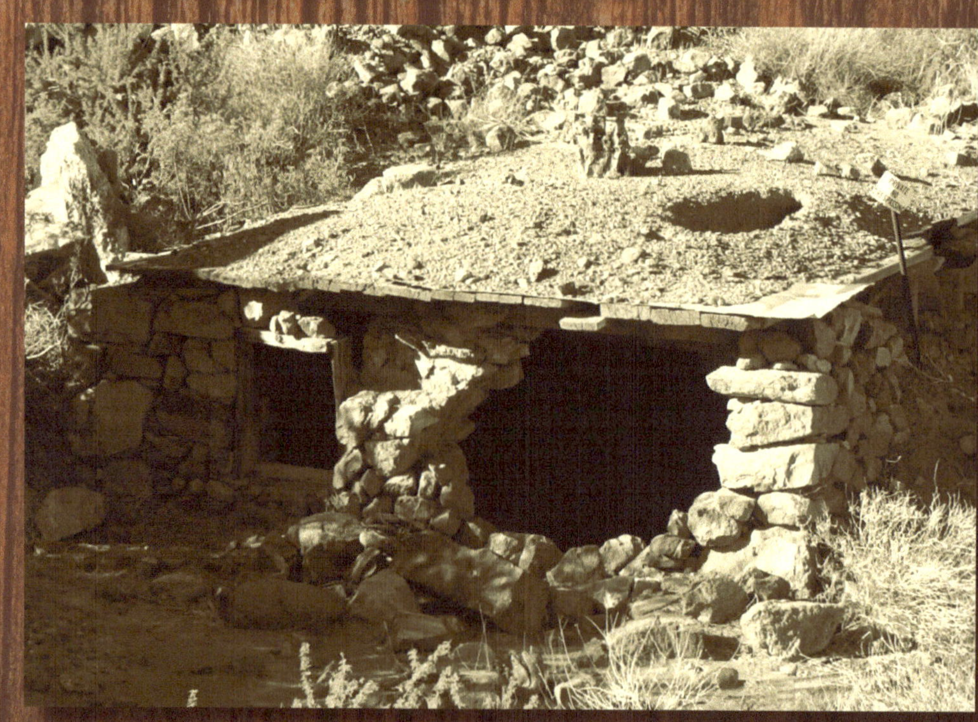

Adult wild burros hang out to be fed carrots, Oatman, Arizona

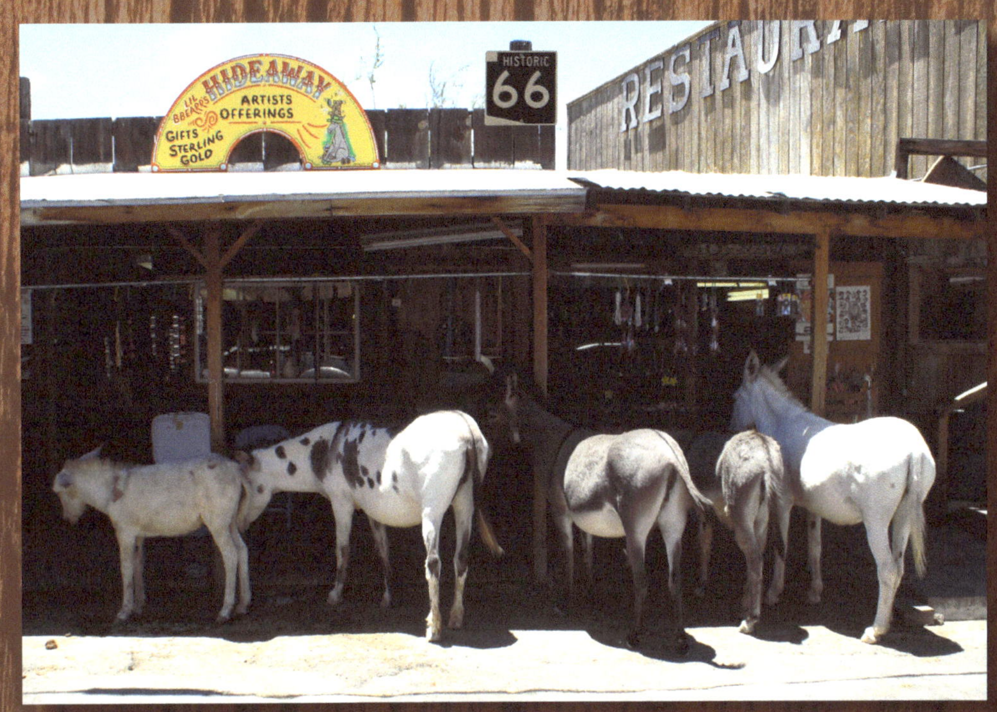

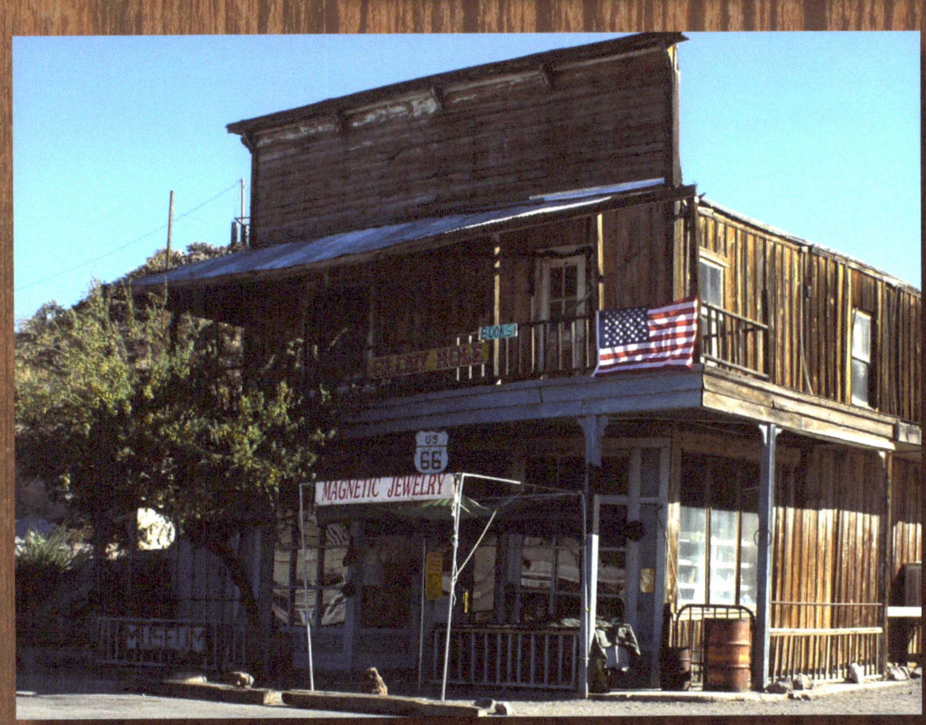

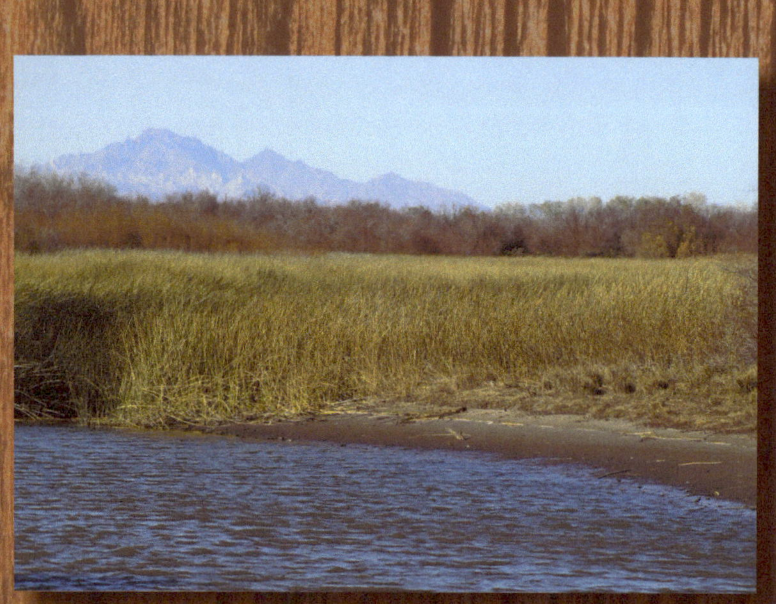

Topock, Marina overlooking part of the Marsh. The Marsh is a protected wild life habitat.

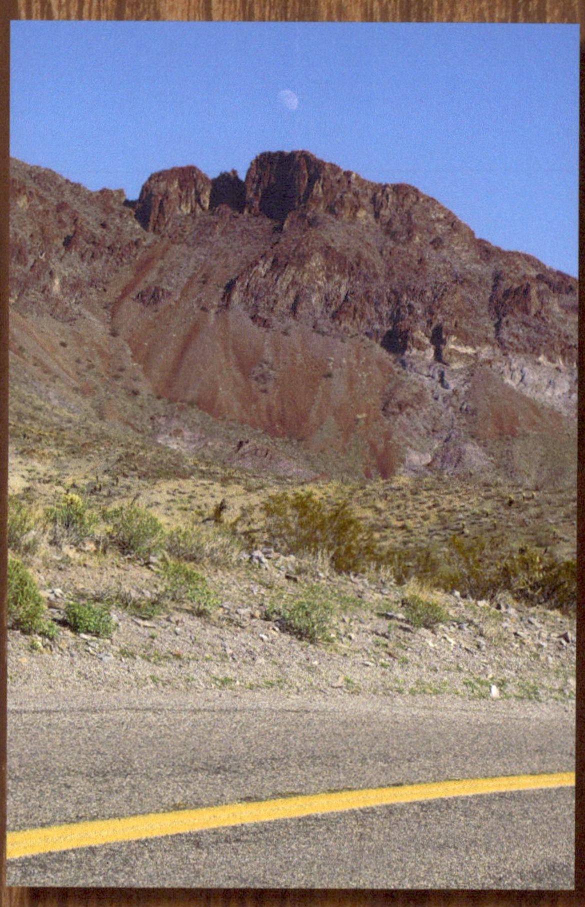

After Topock, Route 66 meets up with Interstate 40.

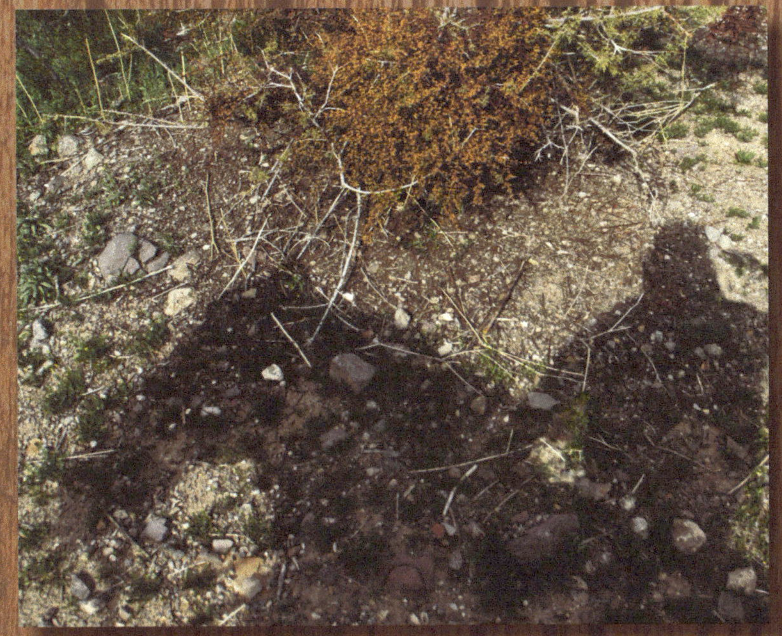

I am my camera's pet human

I started out in Needles, California, in 1966. One really hot place, we're talking 120 degree summers. My dad liked photography, so I did. My first camera/toy was a Browning Reflex. Then I actually got to take real pictures with a Polaroid that did color or black and whites. Black and white was so much cheaper. I annoyed just about everyone I came in contact with because I had some kind of camera all the time.

I traveled Route 66 from Needles to Oklahoma at least twice, as a child and have vividly fond memories of Route 66. I moved to Kingman, in 1984, after having been up to the Hualapai Mountains so often, I felt like a native. Moving to Kingman gave me a whole new set of friends to annoy with my camera.

When someone asks why I take photographs, it is really a concept I have trouble explaining. I guess I want someone to see the beauty that I see and be as amazed as I am. I don't know why we are here or how we came to be, but I am in awe of what exists, whether natural or man-made.

I won my first Editor's Choice award in 2007 from the International Society of Photographers and took a 4th place position at their symposium and convention. I was in a very tough competition and resigned myself to just gaining knowledge. I never expected to place. I owe great thanks to them for the courage they gave me to show off my Photographs.

My name is Herberta Schroeder, I go by Herb, easier to spell and remember, the girl with the guy's name. I am married to a patient man that shares my views on the arts including photography.

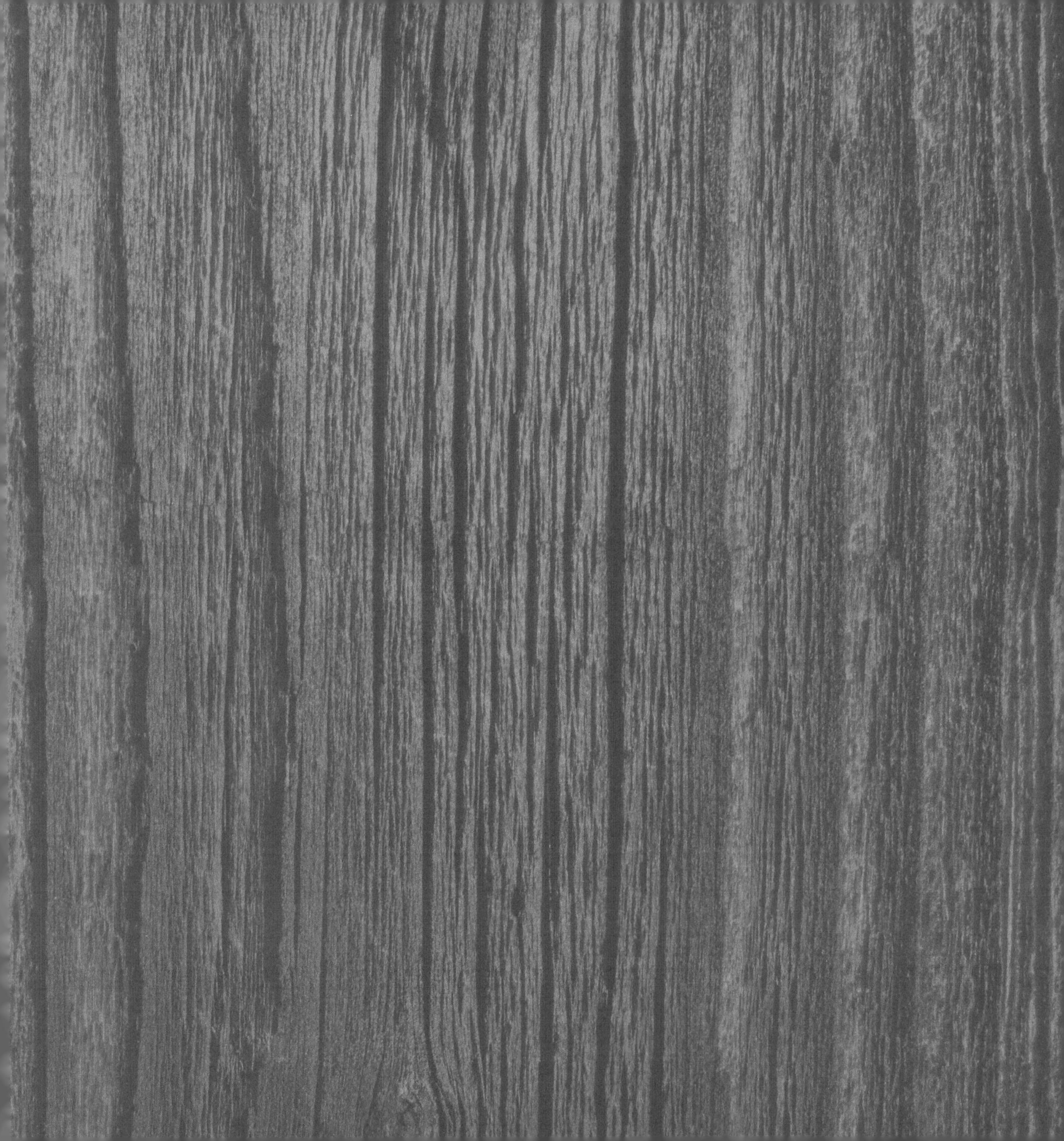

To order prints from this book,
please visit my gallery at

http://www.shutterfly.com/pro/
windsweptimages/rt66

www.ingramcontent.com/pod-product-compliance
Ingram Content Group UK Ltd.
Pitfield, Milton Keynes, MK11 3LW, UK
UKHW060116300726
14090UKWH00002B/217

9781434381361